GEORGE
WASHINGTON

GREAT AMERICAN PRESIDENTS

TABLE OF CONTENTS

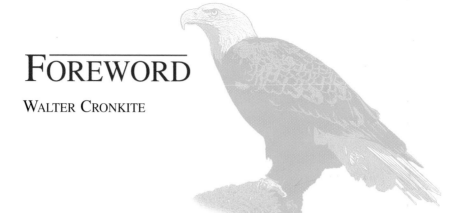

FOREWORD

WALTER CRONKITE

A candle can defy the darkness. It need not have the power of a great searchlight to be a welcome break from the gloom of night. So it goes in the assessment of leadership. He who lights the candle may not have the skill or imagination to turn the light that flickers for a moment into a perpetual glow, but history will assign credit to the degree it is due.

Some of our great American presidents may have had a single moment that bridged the chasm between the ordinary and the exceptional. Others may have assured their lofty place in our history through the sum total of their accomplishments.

When asked who were our greatest presidents, we cannot fail to open our list with the Founding Fathers who put together this nation and nursed it through the difficult years of its infancy. George Washington, John Adams, Thomas Jefferson, and James Madison took the high principles of the revolution against British tyranny and turned the concept of democracy into a nation that became the beacon of hope to oppressed peoples around the globe.

Almost invariably we add to that list our wartime presidents—Abraham Lincoln, perhaps Woodrow Wilson, and certainly Franklin Delano Roosevelt.

Nonetheless there is a thread of irony that runs through the inclusion of the names of those wartime presidents: In many aspects their leadership was enhanced by the fact that, without objection from the people, they assumed extraordinary powers to pursue victory over the nation's enemies (or, in the case of Lincoln, the Southern states).

The complexities of the democratic procedures by which the United States Constitution deliberately tried to withhold unchecked power from the presidency encumbered the presidents who needed their hands freed of the entangling bureaucracy that is the federal government.

Much of our history is written far after the events themselves took place. History may be amended by a much later generation seeking a precedent to justify an action considered necessary at the latter time. The history, in a sense, becomes what later generations interpret it to be.

President Jefferson in 1803 negotiated the purchase of vast lands in the south and west of North America from the French. The deal became knows as the Louisiana Purchase. A century and a half later, to justify seizing the nation's steel mills that were being shut down by a labor strike, President Truman cited the Louisiana Purchase as a case when the president in a major matter ignored Congress and acted almost solely on his own authority.

The case went to the Supreme Court, which overturned Truman six to three. The chief justice, Fred Vinson, was one of the three justices who supported the president. Many historians, however, agreed with the court's majority, pointing out that Jefferson scarcely acted alone: Members of Congress were in the forefront of the agitation to consummate the Louisiana Purchase and Congress voted to fund it.

With more than two centuries of history and precedent now behind us, the Constitution is still found to be flexible when honest and sincere individuals support their own causes with quite different readings of it. These are the questions that end up for interpretation by the Supreme Court.

As late as the early years of the twenty-first century, perhaps the most fateful decision any president ever can make—to commit the nation to war—was again debated and precedent ignored. The Constitution says that only the Congress has the authority to declare war. Yet the Congress, with the objection of few members, ignored this Constitutional provision and voted to give President George W. Bush the right to take the United States to war whenever and under whatever conditions he decided.

Thus a president's place in history may well be determined by how much power he seizes or is granted in re-interpreting and circumventing the remarkable document that is the Constitution. Although the Founding Fathers thought they had spelled out the president's authority in their clear division of powers between the branches of the executive, the legislative and the judiciary, their wisdom has been challenged frequently by ensuing generations. The need and the demand for change is dictated by the march of events, the vast alterations in society, the global condition beyond our influence, and the progress of technology far beyond the imaginations of any of the generations which preceded them.

The extent to which the powers of the presidency will be enhanced and utilized by the chief executives to come in large degree will depend, as they have throughout our history, on the character of the presidents themselves. The limitations on those powers, in turn, will depend on the strength and will of those other two legs of the three-legged stool of American government—the legislative and the judiciary.

And as long as this nation remains a democracy, the final say will rest with an educated electorate in perpetual exercise of its constitutional rights to free speech and a free and alert press.

1

STRIKING FOR FREEDOM

LATE ON THE night of December 25, 1776, a group of cold and tired soldiers began gathering on the Pennsylvania side of the Delaware River. Blocks of ice floated along the water as the soldiers climbed into long black boats in groups of four or five, their movements hidden by darkness. Slowly and clumsily, they loaded 18 field cannons and other artillery, plus the horses required to move them, onto the boats and then pushed off into the river.

Their commander had hoped to complete the crossing of three groups of his men by midnight on that Christmas evening, but as the weather grew more bitter and cold, as the wind blew stronger and sharper and larger blocks of ice formed and blocked the boats,

Washington and a small group of Continental Army soldiers braved stormy weather and rough seas to cross the Delaware River late on the night of December 25, 1776, and surprised a camp of Hessian soldiers in Trenton, New Jersey. The surprise attack, a Continental Army victory, was a turning point in the Revolutionary War.

it became clear that only one group of soldiers would be able to cross the river. The soldiers, using poles to push their boats along the river, were forced to break their way through the ice, trying their best to avoid the larger frozen blocks that could capsize them at any moment. Water splashed up onto them and then froze, making every movement even more difficult.

It was not until 4:00 A.M. on December 26, 1776, that

the boats were unloaded; the horses, artillery, and cannons were assembled; and the men were arranged in formation. They were now facing a nine-mile march to their goal: a camp of German men known as Hessian soldiers who were working for the British army at their post in Trenton, New Jersey. Sunrise was only three hours away. The element of surprise that the commander had hoped to use to his advantage would be gone—2,400 men, 18 cannons, and a large troop of horses would certainly be spotted advancing when the sun rose.

The 44-year-old commander paused as his troops gathered. Should he give up on the planned attack or proceed and hope for the best? As he debated, the storm's intensity increased. Rain, hail, and snow covered the roads. The commander knew, however, that the storm making the march more difficult would also provide cover for his advancing troops. He understood that a retreat would be nearly impossible and even more dangerous than the initial crossing. He gave the order to proceed.

The attack was a desperate move in a war that seemed dangerously one-sided. The group of soldiers crossing the Delaware River that December night was part of the Continental Army. Their leader, the commander in chief of the Continental Army, was the man who had been charged with leading the colonies' war for independence from England: a general named George Washington.

Washington's forces had suffered several humiliating defeats prior to crossing the river. Fighting had been going on for more than a year, and the armed resistance of the colonists seemed to be a poor match for the polished and well-trained British army. The Continental forces lacked weapons, their clothes were in rags, and they were badly in need of even the most basic supplies—things like food, shoes, blankets, and tents. Worse still, the Continental Army was made up largely of militia (citizens organized for military service) from the various colonies. They were men who had signed up to fight for a fixed period of time—a period of time that was due to expire at the end of the year, only a few days away.

This ragged bunch of soldiers presented a dismal picture to the citizens who remained undecided in the conflict with England. Many took one look at the desperate, weary men marching through the streets, compared them with the well-armed, brilliantly clothed professional British soldiers, and quickly decided which side would win. The British forces, commanded by General William Howe, published a statement offering all colonists a full pardon if they would turn over their weapons and return to their homes within 60 days. It was an attractive offer to the sick and exhausted soldiers, and Washington knew that he had to act quickly before his army fell apart.

Between 2,000 and 3,000 Hessian soldiers were thought to be holding the village of Trenton—a town of about 100 homes, many of which stood empty—with no British troops in the immediate vicinity. Washington's spies had informed him that the Hessians had only six field cannons and that the main British strongholds were farther north, at Princeton.

By 8:00 A.M., Washington's army had slipped and slid its way along the road to arrive at the prearranged formation. They had been ordered to attack as soon as they arrived at a point about half a mile outside the Trenton camp. The plan was to catch the Hessians by surprise when they were still asleep after a night of Christmas celebration, to force them from the houses they were occupying and then, by blocking the bridge across the Assunpink Creek, to cut off their only line of retreat.

The Continental soldiers were finally spotted by an advance guard, who shouted a warning. The Hessians stumbled from their beds and emerged to a round of fire from the Continental forces, who were still too far off to hit their targets. There was much noise and confusion, and the driving snow made it difficult for the Hessians to see who was firing at them. They only knew that they were under attack. They tried to return the fire, but the storm blinded them.

The Hessians soon retreated, keeping up a volley of covering fire as they pulled back. The American forces, some running, others sliding on the icy paths, chased them. General Washington personally led a group of soldiers forward. The Hessians soon found themselves surrounded, blocked on three sides by American forces and on the other by the icy Assunpink Creek. Their artillery had been seized, and sleet and hail were falling, making it impossible for them to see to get into the formations in which they had been trained to fight.

The Hessians put down their weapons and surrendered.

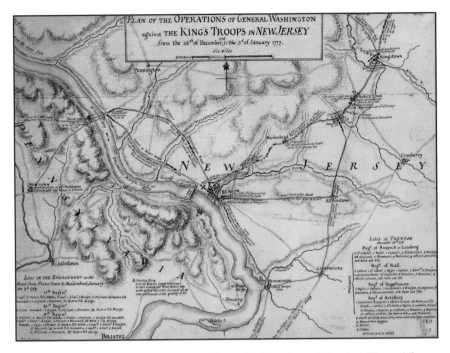

Washington carefully planned the attack on the Hessians at Trenton. The soldiers, mercenaries for the British army, surrendered after finding themselves surrounded on three sides by American troops and on the fourth by the Assunpink Creek. Washington followed this success with other surprise attacks, such as the one on Princeton.

Less than two hours had passed, and the Continental Army, only a few days from being disbanded, had won its greatest victory. Not a single American life had been lost.

As the news of the Hessian surrender was confirmed, George Washington turned to one of his officers. "This is a glorious day for our country," he said.

A NEW KIND OF WAR

The Battle at Trenton marked a crucial turning point for the Revolutionary War and for the skilled commander in chief of the Continental forces. George Washington had struggled to motivate his soldiers as they suffered defeat after defeat. The skills of the professional British soldiers offered a marked contrast to the Colonial forces. Their weapons and their supplies were vastly superior. Washington, however, knew that men fighting for their homes, their families, and their freedom would fight harder and longer than men fighting for a paycheck. He also knew that the British army had a significant weakness: It was prepared to fight in specific ways at specific times. Few British commanders would have thought to attempt to lead troops across icy water in a driving snowstorm or to order their soldiers to break formation and fight hidden behind trees, hills, and buildings like snipers.

Washington had observed these tactics win success for Native American Indian warriors when he had served in a different army—the British army—years earlier during the French and Indian War. He knew that his soldiers were familiar with the weather conditions and the hills and forests of their country and that they could use the element of surprise to prevent their enemies from falling into the formations critical for a British victory. The tactic worked brilliantly at Trenton and would be used more often to finally force the end of British rule in the American colonies.

The victory at Trenton was merely the beginning of a new offensive against the British forces. Washington would lead another unexpected attack on the British stronghold of Princeton. These successes provided more than an opportunity to demonstrate American determination to continue the fight and to seize prisoners of war and their supplies and artillery; they also prevented the colony of New Jersey from surrendering completely to British control and ensured that Philadelphia would remain safe for that winter. Perhaps most important of all, they demonstrated to the citizens of the American colonies that the fight for independence was still strong and encouraged soldiers whose terms of service were about to expire that there was hope—hope that inspired them to re-enlist and continue the fight.

The victories at Trenton and Princeton added to George Washington's reputation as a superior military commander. The successes renewed the faith of his temporary army and of the citizens he would lead one day.

"Much! Very much, indeed, is it to be lamented that when Men are brought to play the part of Soldiers thus well, that any of them, for the sake of a little temporary ease, should think of abandoning the cause of Liberty and their Country at so important a crisis."
— From George Washington's orders to his men, written on December 27, 1776, shortly after their victory at Trenton, to encourage his men to re-enlist

A LEGENDARY LEADER

George Washington is a familiar figure to most Americans. His face appears on the one-dollar bill. He is described as the "Father of Our Country" and as the fearless leader of the Revolutionary Army. The legends and stories that surround George Washington, however, have at times painted a false picture of one of the greatest American presidents. He is remembered for chopping down a cherry tree or for wearing false wooden teeth. His "birthday," once a national holiday, has now been changed to "Presidents Day," falling for the convenience of school and business calendars on the third Monday in February. (Washington was actually born on February 11, 1732. During his lifetime, the calendar was changed, shifting his birthday ahead 11 days to February 22.)

When we picture George Washington, we are left with legends and the portraits painted of him. Perhaps the most famous, painted by the well-known artist Gilbert Stuart, focuses unflatteringly on Washington's mouth and the odd shape caused by his large dentures. Stuart did not like Washington: He found him too stiff and formal and too unwilling to recognize Stuart's talent as a portrait painter. Stuart created a picture of an unsmiling old man that has permanently tainted our thoughts of this great leader.

George Washington is much more than cherry trees and false teeth. He is more than a commander leading an army across the icy Delaware River on a Christmas night. By serving as the first president of the United States, he would dramatically and permanently create a mold for all future presidents. He would shape the government upon which the United States would be built, helping to establish the separation of powers, the strength of the executive branch, and the role of president as commander in chief of the armed forces. It was with George Washington in mind that much of the function of the American president was first created. His example lives on in the practice of peaceful succession of popularly elected presidents, in the two-term

George Washington was a reluctant politician, but he always served his country when asked. By serving as the first president of the United States, he helped shape the presidency, ensuring the strength of the executive branch. The office of the president was created with Washington in mind, and thus Washington is the model for all presidents who have followed.

presidential limit, and in the way the country was unified from a group of 13 very different, independent colonies.

We remember George Washington as a great leader, perhaps the best choice for our first president and the man best equipped to lead the United States. Still, George Washington suffered many of the same problems our presidents do today: criticism from the media, rival politicians attempting to get rid of him, cabinet members crippled by scandals, the threat of war, and the challenges of governing vast territories of very different people.

To understand why George Washington is remembered as one of the greatest American presidents, it is important to learn more about him as a man, a military leader, a reluctant politician, and a citizen. At many moments throughout Washington's life, the decisions he wrestled with were the same decisions confronting his fellow citizens. Should he remain loyal to his king, the king he had served as a soldier in the British army? Should he stay at home to farm his land or go off to fight? Could he survive the harsh conditions, the lack of supplies, and the threat of smallpox and other diseases?

Once the war was won and independence was achieved, Washington's decisions shaped the new nation. He chose not to accept the pleas that he become king of the United States. He instead helped draft a government made up of unified, rather than independent, states, with popularly elected leaders and a system of checks and balances that would ensure that no group became too powerful. He reluctantly agreed to become the new nation's president but wisely resisted a lifetime appointment, instead retiring after two terms despite the urging of most citizens that he remain in power. Then, retiring to his home in Mount Vernon, Virginia, he quietly and systematically put the plans in place to free his slaves upon his death.

George Washington was a brilliant leader, a skillful commander, a gifted politician, and an extraordinary man. His life offers a glimpse of a new nation at the moment of its creation, and his contributions largely shaped the country that would become the United States.

2

THE YOUNG SOLDIER

IN MARCH OF 1748, Lord Thomas Fairfax learned that squatters were living on his land. Lord Fairfax was one of the wealthiest men in the American colony of Virginia, and his plantation stretched across five million acres of land, a territory so vast that not even he knew precisely where it began or ended. He decided that clear boundaries needed to be mapped out and then marked along his land, so that he could make it clear to any would-be settlers that they were entering private property.

He hired his 16-year-old neighbor, a hardworking young man named George Washington, to go with a guide and map out his property. George needed the job, and he welcomed the

George Washington inherited Mount Vernon, the family's modest tobacco farm, when his older half brother Lawrence died in 1752. Washington's father, Augustine, had settled the farm, and when he died, the estate amounted to 10,000 acres of land and 50 slaves.

opportunity to make his first trip into the western wilderness. His father had died when George was only 11 years old, leaving most of his property to George's half brother Lawrence.

George explored the territory for the next month.

He slept outdoors and caught his food using only a small pocketknife. He saw Indians and traders and the primitive conditions of settlers. He kept a journal of his trip in a small notebook. In one journal entry, he wrote, "Rain'd till about two oClock & Clear'd when we were agreeably surpris'd at the sight of thirty odd Indians coming from War with only one Scalp."

George was thus able to learn the trade of surveying firsthand, and the knowledge that he gained during the trip about the wilderness that made up the western frontier of the American colonies helped shape his future careers as a surveyor, a soldier, and ultimately as president.

Washington spent the next few years working as a surveyor mapping out the land that marked the colony of Virginia. He was careful with the money he earned and soon had saved enough to buy more than 1,400 acres of land beyond the Blue Ridge Mountains. At the age of 18, he was well on his way to building a successful career.

Tragic events soon forced him to change his plans. His older half brother, whom Washington adored, became sick from consumption. In those days, it was thought that a change of climate could help, so Washington traveled with Lawrence to the tropical island of Barbados in the Caribbean Sea in search of a cure. In Barbados, Washington himself became ill, suffering from an attack of smallpox. The two sick brothers did their best to take care of each other while far from home, and ultimately George did recover. His illness would later prove lucky: The attack was relatively mild, and it gave him immunity to a disease that would become a major killer during the American Revolution.

Lawrence was not so lucky. He died in 1752, leaving George to inherit the family property known as Mount Vernon.

A MODEST BEGINNING

The Mount Vernon that we know today is far grander than the modest plantation that Washington's father had built overlooking the Potomac River. George's great-grandfather, John Washington, had immigrated to the American colonies from northern England in 1657 and settled near the Potomac. The colony of Virginia was only about 50 years old at the time, and John Washington prospered there, marrying the daughter of a wealthy tobacco planter and becoming himself a wealthy planter.

John Washington's sons and grandsons followed his example, choosing wealthy women as their brides, building their own plantations, and growing tobacco. George Washington's father, Augustine Washington, was no exception. He married twice; by the time he died at the age of 49, his property included about 10,000 acres of land and 50 slaves.

In today's terms, we would describe Washington's family as middle class. They were not nearly as wealthy as many of their Virginia neighbors. George was born in a four-room farmhouse near the Potomac River called Ferry's Farm. His father later built the larger house at Mount Vernon, but when Augustine Washington died,

Lawrence inherited Mount Vernon, and George, his mother, and his three younger brothers and sisters were forced to move back to Ferry's Farm.

The death of George's father when George was only 11 meant that many of the advantages his older half brothers had enjoyed would not be possible for him. George had hoped to go to school in England, as his father and half brothers had. It was a deep disappointment to him that the family could not afford to send him away. Instead, his formal education ended when he was about 15 years old.

Lawrence, who was 14 years older than George, seemed to have received all of the advantages. As an English-educated gentleman and property owner, he married the daughter of his wealthy neighbors, the Fairfaxes. He was appointed to an important position in Virginia's militia and was elected to Virginia's legislative assembly, the House of Burgesses.

Lawrence was determined to help the younger brother who adored him, and he would become the most important influence on George Washington's life. Much of what George would accomplish early in life would be the result of either Lawrence's assistance or his influence.

A DIPLOMATIC MISSION

Lawrence had served briefly in the British military and told George colorful tales of his experiences, so it is not surprising that shortly after Lawrence's death, George decided to follow in his brother's footsteps and seek a military position. At the time, Virginia was divided into military districts, and George was finally appointed a major of the smallest before winning the right to serve over his own home district.

He continued surveying, traveling through the Shenandoah Valley and earning a good salary and a reputation for fair and honest work. This combination of a surveyor's knowledge of the frontier and military service would mark Washington's entry into a war that would shape America's future.

France and England had spent a good part of the 1700s competing for power and influence, and the vast stretches of land in America became yet another source of conflict between the two powerful nations. French explorers were the first to discover the Mississippi River, and they claimed that land for France, building forts that stretched from the St. Lawrence River (along the U.S. border with Canada) south to the Gulf of Mexico. England, however, claimed that its 13 colonies included this territory, because when the colonies were first chartered they were described as stretching from "sea to sea" (beginning at the Atlantic Ocean and stretching west to the Pacific Ocean, although it would be many years before the true vastness of the North American continent was understood and explored).

Both the British and French enlisted the help of Indians to help them fight battles for the land. The French had been better friends to the Indians: The British cut down forests and cleared land for tobacco and other products, which destroyed Indian hunting grounds and forced them farther west. The French, on the other hand, had focused more on exploring and trading, living relatively peacefully among the Indians without drastically disturbing their way of life. When it came time to choose sides between these two countries, it is not surprising that most Indians chose to help the French.

In 1752, a conflict broke out when George II, the king of England, gave a group of important Virginians the right to plant thousands of acres in the territory known as Ohio. The group, known as the Ohio Company, sent out explorers to map the land and begin to build roads.

The Ohio Company faced a major problem almost from the beginning: The land King George II had generously given to them was not unexplored wilderness but instead was the home to Indian tribes. In addition, French soldiers had built forts in the region.

When the problem was explained to King George, his solution was simple: He ordered the French to leave. If the French refused, the British would use force to retake what the king said was their soil.

There were not many men who wanted to deliver that message to the French. Not only would the French be unlikely to welcome the message or the messenger, but also the task would involve traveling across hundreds of miles of unmapped forests and mountains, in which hostile Indian tribes might attack, in the middle of winter.

One man, learning of the mission, hurried to Virginia's capital, Williamsburg, to volunteer. George Washington later noted that it was unusual that someone as young and

Washington, portrayed here as a young land surveyor, became familiar with the wilderness through his work. This knowledge is one reason he was selected to carry a message from the king of England to the French occupying land in the Ohio Territory in 1752. His report on this journey made him famous in the colonies and in England.

inexperienced as he was would be given such an important task, but he offered a number of important qualifications: He was a Virginia property owner with a military commission, who had spent years surveying rugged and dangerous territory. He had some knowledge of the Indians, and at 6'3", he was a tall and impressive figure, one who seemed worthy to carry a message from the king of England.

FIRST EXPERIENCE OF FAME

It took more than a month of travel across difficult terrain for Washington and his small group of frontiersmen to reach the French fort and present the king's orders to the French commander. The commander treated Washington with politeness but explained that a British king could not issue orders to France.

Washington knew that he needed to return quickly to Williamsburg with this response. The journey back, however, was even more difficult than the initial trip. The exhausted horses could no longer travel and the frontiersmen who had traveled with him gave up. In the end, Washington traveled with only one guide, hurrying through deep snow and freezing temperatures to reach Williamsburg in January of 1754.

The governor of Virginia asked Washington to provide him with a report in writing. Washington spent the next 24 hours summarizing his experiences, which would be printed and circulated in England and in the American colonies under the title

---

December 23, 1753:

". . . The Horses grew less able to travel every Day; the Cold increased very fast; and the Roads were becoming much worse by a deep Snow, continually freezing. . . . I determined to prosecute my Journey the nearest Way through the Woods, on Foot . . . .

". . . Just after we had passed a Place called the Murdering-Town . . . we fell in with a Party of French Indians, who had lain in Wait for us. One of them fired at Mr. Gist or me, not 15 steps off, but fortunately missed. We took this Fellow into Custody, and kept him till about 9 o'clock at Night; Then let him go, and walked all the remaining Part of the Night without making any Stop; that we might get the Start, so far, as to be out of the Reach of their Pursuit the next Day, since we were well assured that they would follow our Tract as soon it was light . . . ."

— From *The Journal of Major George Washington, Sent . . . to the Commandant of the French Forces on the Ohio*

The Journal of Major George Washington, Sent . . . to the Commandant of the French Forces on the Ohio. With this one mission, Washington became famous in both England and the colonies.

EMBARRASSMENT AT FORT NECESSITY

The governor of Virginia decided to use force to drive the French out of their settlement in the Ohio country. Once again confronted by a difficult mission, he chose George Washington.

Washington set out in April of 1754, this time with a promotion and in command of more than 150 soldiers. His orders were to occupy the strategically critical Forks of the Ohio—the point where the Allegheny and Monongahela Rivers merged to form the Ohio River. As Washington traveled west, he learned that the Forks of the Ohio was already occupied—by more than a thousand French soldiers.

On May 28, 1754, Washington discovered a small party of French soldiers camping in the woods. Shots were soon fired, and 10 French soldiers (including their commander) were killed. The survivors then explained that they were on a diplomatic mission, sent (as Washington had been a few months earlier) to carry a message demanding that the British withdraw from French territory. The incident became known as the Jumonville Affair.

This tiny skirmish between two small groups of soldiers in a remote part of the American wilderness would spark a worldwide conflict. The French claimed that

Washington had murdered an ambassador; Washington insisted that he had defended himself against a group of soldiers who had intended to attack him. These differing views of a small battle would ultimately push England and France into an escalating conflict that by 1756 would erupt in war. The war, which Americans know as the French and Indian War, would be labeled the Seven Years' War by the rest of the world and would stretch beyond the American territories, beyond the borders of England and France, to include battles in Russia, Spain, Portugal, Austria, Prussia, and Germany.

As the conflict was building, Washington continued in his effort to establish a military presence at the Forks of the Ohio. Promoted to colonel, he built a fort—known as Fort Necessity—about 50 miles away. The spot he chose for Fort Necessity was one a more experienced soldier would never have selected: The land was situated downhill, in an exposed clearing.

Washington was waiting for reinforcements when the fort was attacked by a group of Indians and French soldiers. Rain poured down, making it difficult for Washington's men to keep their gunpowder dry. Snipers hidden in the hills killed nearly one-third of Washington's men before he was forced to surrender.

The French allowed the Virginians to take their weapons from the fort and return home. They had only one demand: George Washington had to sign a "document of surrender." Washington signed the paper, written in French, a language he didn't understand. It was only later that he would learn that he had signed a statement admitting that he had assassinated a French ambassador.

Washington returned to Virginia embarrassed by the defeat and because his signing of the admission gave the French an important tool to use in propaganda. He had disobeyed the orders he had been given to a fight only if the French first attacked. Washington went home to Mount Vernon feeling sick and humiliated.

A COLONIAL HERO

Many in England viewed Washington's defeat as typical of what they felt were inferior Colonial forces. There was a strong bias against Colonial soldiers; George Washington had often been angry at the favoritism shown in the English military, in which any English officer was considered to outrank a Colonial officer, even a Colonial colonel commanding an entire regiment.

As war became more likely, the king of England decided to send out one of his most experienced British officers—Major General Edward Braddock—along with a huge expeditionary force designed to prove once and for all to the French exactly who controlled the Ohio territory. The expedition was to set out in early 1755. Washington was eager to redeem himself and soon offered to assist Braddock. Braddock knew that Washington's experience in the region and his knowledge of the enemy would be useful and accepted the offer.

By the summer, Braddock had nearly reached the disputed Forks territory. His forces numbered 2,000 British soldiers plus another 500 Colonial soldiers. Braddock was confident that his superior forces could quickly seize the Forks and then move on to capture other French forts in the region in a demonstration of British power.

Braddock accepted Washington's advice on which routes to take, but he ignored Washington's cautions about the very different style of fighting the Indians used. Braddock shared the British contempt for Colonial soldiers: He felt that they had been poorly trained and knew little of the discipline that was a key to British military success. The British soldiers, in their bright red uniforms, were taught to fight in long, even lines, with two enemies marching steadily toward each other and then exchanging fire before charging with their bayonets.

Washington tried to warn the general that the French soldiers he would encounter had accustomed themselves to the Indian style of battle: They would not announce their presence in advance but would instead use the element of surprise to ambush soldiers, attacking quickly with loud war whoops or shooting at their enemies while safely hidden by trees or hills. Braddock ignored the advice, deciding to split off 1,500 of his men and lead them in an attack on the French Fort Duquesne.

Washington was fighting off an illness, but when he learned of the plan he decided to ride with Braddock's forces to witness the fort's capture. What he saw would become one of England's most embarrassing and unexpected defeats.

On July 9, 1755, the force of 1,500 British soldiers was

On July 9, 1755, Major General Edward Braddock and 1,500 British soldiers on the way to attack Fort Duquesne, a French fort, were ambushed by French and Indian forces. Washington had warned Braddock about the Indian fighting style that the French used, hiding themselves in the wilderness and using surprise attacks. This was one of England's worst defeats during the French and Indian War.

attacked by a few hundred French soldiers and Indian warriors. Braddock's forces had no advance notice before they were suddenly being shot and killed by enemies, who were safely hidden behind the trees and bushes. Washington urged Braddock to order the men to hide themselves behind the trees, but Braddock refused to allow his men to break rank. Washington rode among the Virginia troops—the only ones who had any experience fighting this "invisible" enemy—urging them to keep fighting. Two horses were shot down from under him and bullets tore his coat and hat, but still Washington did his best to prevent his men from panicking.

The battle ended quickly. More than half of Braddock's men were wounded or killed; Braddock himself was shot and died a few days later. The remains of the British army retreated to Philadelphia. Washington traveled back to Williamsburg, where he discovered that the city was stunned by the defeat but full of stories of Washington's bravery during the battle. He was once more a hero.

VICTORY IN THE FRENCH AND INDIAN WAR

Washington spent the next three years in command of a column of Colonial militia. Forced to make do with few trained soldiers and scarce supplies, he was frustrated by a bureaucracy (a group of government officials and advisers) that was often ill informed of the realities of battle. At the same time, he learned to lead and inspire and gained experience both in commanding and in the military tactics that worked best on American soil. All of these experiences would shape him into the Revolutionary War general he would become.

In 1758, Washington's troops enjoyed the triumph of finally overpowering the French and driving them from the fort on the Forks of the Ohio, the fort that had contributed to the start of the French and Indian War. The French set the fort on fire as they fled, but a new fort would be built in its place—an English fort that was named Fort Pitt in honor of William Pitt, the prime minister of England. The town that grew up around that fort would take its name and become known first as Pittsborough and later as Pittsburgh.

Satisfied that his honor was fully restored and his most important military objective—to force the French from the Forks of the Ohio—had finally been achieved, Washington resigned from military service. At the age of 26, he was looking forward to spending the remainder of his life in quiet retirement, managing his farm at Mount Vernon.

3

THE
COLONIES
UNITE

ON JANUARY 6, 1759, Colonel George Washington married a wealthy young widow named Martha Custis and became the stepfather of her two young children. The marriage brought more than happiness and companionship to Washington: It also brought added wealth and property, because Martha's first husband had left a substantial estate.

Washington was now a member of the Virginia upper class and was chosen to join the legislature that helped govern the Virginia colony: the House of Burgesses. Washington began his first session in Williamsburg on his 27th birthday. The most important men in Virginia held seats in the House of Burgesses,

Washington married Martha Custis, a widow, on January 6, 1759, and became a stepfather to her two children. Martha's first husband had left a sizable estate, and the Washingtons became part of Virginia's upperclass.

and yet after only four days there, Washington was embarrassed when a resolution was offered: ". . . that the thanks of the House be given to George Washington, Esq; a member of this House, late Colonel of the First Virginia Regiment, for his faithful Services to his

Majesty, and this Colony, and for his brave and steady behavior. . . ."

Washington spent the next several years enjoying life on his farm and focusing on making it profitable. Like most Virginia planters, the crop he chose was tobacco. Also like most Virginia planters, Washington purchased slaves to work on his plantation. As he neared the end of his life, Washington would become disturbed by slavery and by his own participation in such a terrible system, but it is important not to overlook the fact that he owned slaves.

Washington's efforts to raise a profitable tobacco crop met with failure. At that time, British merchants had a monopoly on the tobacco crops of Virginia and also enjoyed a monopoly on much of the trade in the colony. Most farms in Virginia were tobacco farms. The goods that colonists needed—seeds, cloth, tea, flour, sugar, china, books, and so on—all were shipped to the colonists by British merchants overseas. There was very little trade from one colony to another; each colony was viewed as a separate settlement, linked more to England than to the other colonies.

Despite his wealth, Washington soon found himself in debt to British merchants. He was not the only Virginia planter in debt, but unlike many of his neighbors, he decided to do something about it. Ignoring the British policy that encouraged all Virginia farmers to focus on tobacco, Washington decided to find a crop better suited to the soil at Mount Vernon. After spending several years testing different agricultural methods and different plant-ings, Washington found a crop that worked: wheat.

It was a small step toward independence from British control. Washington was able to pay off his debt and to offer his neighbors a crop that they needed at a price they could afford. Mount Vernon quickly became a successful farm. Washington was able to add to his estates, buying the land that was available along the Ohio Valley once the French and Indian War ended in 1763.

The end of the war, however, brought more to the colonists than newly available land along the western frontier. It brought taxes.

TAXES RAISE A DISPUTE

The seven years of war had been very costly for England, and the debt of the war was crushing. In England, the argument was made that the colonists had benefited the most from the war, so the colonists should pay for it. In 1760, a new king, George III, had taken the throne and he agreed.

In 1765, the British Parliament passed a tax known as the Stamp Act. It required colonists to pay a kind of sales tax on any items that carried a special stamp—things like newspapers, playing cards, writing paper, and special legal documents such as bills, licenses, and property deeds.

The Stamp Act affected all of the colonies, and for the first time, they found themselves united in protest against what many viewed as an unjust tax. Colonists did not have a representative in the British Parliament, so they thought it was unfair for this same Parliament to be able to pass laws taxing them. "No taxation without representation" became the popular response to the Stamp Act. A year later, following protests, boycotts, and even violent riots, Parliament was forced to repeal the Stamp Act. The king was furious at the protests and decided to bring the colonies back under control. The colonists, however, had learned that they might have more in common with each other than with a distant country on the other side of the Atlantic Ocean.

In 1767, another tax—a tax on imported goods—was passed. The tax, known as the Townshend Acts, forced colonists to pay an additional sum for things like glass, lead, paper, and tea. The assembly in Massachusetts called on the other colonies to join in their protest of this "unconstitutional" tax.

In response, the Massachusetts assembly was dissolved and British troops were ordered to move into Boston. Colonists in New York, Philadelphia, and Boston responded by boycotting all goods imported from England.

Washington had not been very vocal when the Townshend Acts were first passed, but by April 1769, as British troops moved into Boston and the American assemblies were clearly under threat, he became one of the first to call for action. In a letter to his neighbor, George Mason, Washington made clear his belief that British policies were deliberately attacking the freedom of the colonists and that independence was the only solution that would work.

In his letter, Washington also began to consider the possibility that the colonists might have to take up arms to achieve independence.

RESPONSE TO THE INTOLERABLE ACTS

Parliament was ultimately forced to repeal most of the Townshend Acts. Only one tax was left in place: a three-penny-a-pound tax on tea, but colonists continued to protest the remaining tax. Many merchants refused to carry the taxed tea, and in Boston on December 16, 1773, a group disguised as Indians dumped 50 tons of British tea into Boston Harbor. This incident became known as the Boston Tea Party.

"April 5, 1769

At a time when our lordly Masters in Great Britain will be satisfied with nothing less than the deprication of American freedom, it seems highly necessary that some thing shou'd be done to avert the stroke and maintain the liberty which we have derived from our Ancestors. . . .

"That no man shou'd scruple, or hesitate a moment to use arms in defence of so valuable a blessing, on which all the good and evil of life depends; is clearly my opinion; yet Arms I wou'd beg leave to add, should be the last resource . . . ."

— George Washington, in a letter to neighbor George Mason, in which Washington shared his belief that the colonies might need to break from England and fight for their independence

England refused to allow this kind of outright rebellion and targeted Massachusetts as the source of all protests against British law. Parliament passed a series of laws designed to punish the Massachusetts colony for its rebellion—laws that came to be known in the colonies as the Intolerable Acts. The laws prevented any trade from coming into Boston Harbor. The colony's charter

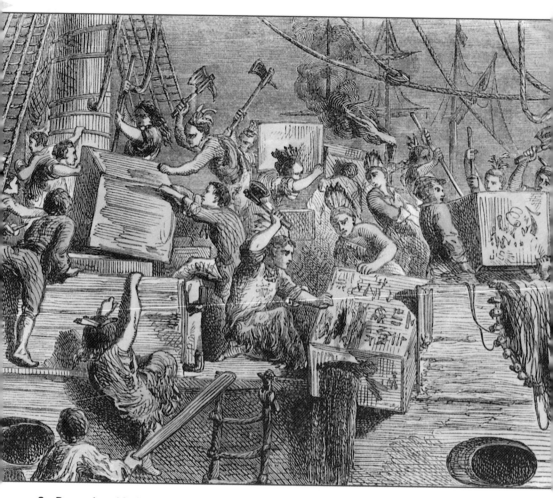

On December 16, 1773, in an incident known as the Boston Tea Party, a group of men disguised as Indians boarded British ships and dumped their cargo, 50 tons of tea, into Boston Harbor in protest of the British tax on tea. Taxation in the colonies was unpopular because the colonies were not represented in the British Parliament.

was revoked, and the British general Thomas Gage was named royal governor of Massachusetts. British warships occupied the harbor, and British troops occupied the city.

Washington was at the House of Burgesses in Williamsburg in May 1774 when the assembly learned of the Intolerable Acts and what was happening in Massachusetts. The assembly called for a day of fasting and prayer to protest the events, and the governor of Virginia, representing the British Crown, quickly responded to the colonists by announcing that the House of Burgesses was dissolved.

The members left the House of Burgesses and moved to a nearby tavern. There, they announced their support for the colonists in Massachusetts and called for a meeting, or "congress," of representatives from all of the colonies.

THE CONTINENTAL ARMY

The delegates chosen to represent the colony of Virginia at the meeting in Philadelphia were an impressive group. Peyton Randolph was a skilled speaker, trained in parliamentary procedures. Richard Henry Lee was an expert on law and government. George Washington was the third delegate selected, nominated both for his military background and for his prestige in the colony. The group from Virginia also included Patrick Henry, Richard Bland, Benjamin Harrison, and Edmund Pendleton.

The First Continental Congress met in Philadelphia— then the largest city in North America—in September 1774. Its principal act was to pass a resolution declaring that the right to dictate internal policy and pass taxes in

America remained within the power of each colony, not with the British Parliament. At this early stage, there was not a sense of America as a new nation. Instead, the representatives felt their greatest loyalty was to their home colony and that each individual colony should hold the right to govern its residents.

Washington made a favorable impression on the other delegates, even though he was neither the most outspoken nor the most passionate. Many were simply amazed at how young he was, expecting the hero of the French and Indian War to be older than 42.

In March 1775, Washington was elected to serve again as one of Virginia's delegates, this time to the Second Continental Congress. By the time the delegates gathered in Philadelphia, the mood in the colonies had grown even more hostile. Battles at Lexington and Concord indicated that war between the British and the colonists was almost inevitable. A division of the Massachusetts militia had managed to occupy Bunker Hill, but the delegates from Massachusetts made it clear that they needed the other colonies to support them in their efforts.

Washington understood that the time had come for colonists to make a choice. He made this clear when he strode into the Second Continental Congress dressed in his militia uniform. The delegates from Massachusetts were grateful for this demonstration of Washington's attitude. Up until now, the fighting had been almost exclusively between England and Massachusetts.

Washington was one of Virginia's delegates to the Second Continental Congress in Philadelphia, where he was given command of the Massachusetts militia, renamed the Continental Army. He had worn his military uniform to the Congress to show Virginia's support for Massachusetts, where much of the colonial rebellion had taken place.

The support of the politically vital Virginia colony was critical to ensure that it wasn't simply Massachusetts' rebellion.

The Second Continental Congress acted to name the militia in Massachusetts as the "Continental Army." The army needed a commander, and Washington was the unanimous choice. Washington was chosen for his military reputation and also as a demonstration that the colonies should be united: The militia in Massachusetts now had a Virginian general (the Congress gave Washington a promotion to go along with the new post). Washington humbly accepted the command, refusing a salary and asking only that the Congress pay any expenses he might have.

> *"Though I am truly sensible of the high honor done me, in this appointment, yet I feel great distress, from a consciousness that my abilities and military experience may not be equal to the extensive and important trust. However, as the Congress desire it, I will enter upon the momentous duty, and exert every power I possess in their service, and for the support of the glorious cause . . . . But, lest some unlucky event should happen. . . I beg it may be remembered by every gentleman in the room, that I, this day, declare with the utmost sincerity, I do not think myself equal to the command I am honored with."*
>
> — From Washington's speech at the Second Continental Congress, demonstrating both a sense of duty and an awareness of the importance of the task after he was the unanimous choice to serve as commander of the new Continental Army

Washington then wrote to his wife to explain his new command and drew up a will. He headed for Boston, where he took command of the new Continental Army on July 3, 1775. The 15,000 militiamen that formed

Washington's forces were disorganized, undisciplined, and untrained. A congress in faraway Philadelphia had called them an army. Washington had to make them one. Then he had to lead them into battle against one of the most powerful armies in the world.

4

THE REVOLUTION BEGINS

THE NEW GENERAL of the Continental Army was faced with a daunting task. His army was much smaller than he had hoped; he needed better supplies, more tents, and more food. His men needed uniforms, or at least decent clothing. They needed better medical facilities, better artillery, and more skilled officers.

Somehow, despite these disadvantages, the Continental Army managed to hold on to its position. In March 1776, under heavy fire from Continental artillery, the British left Boston. The citizens of Massachusetts celebrated the victory with great joy, but Washington understood that the British had not given up—they

John Hancock defiantly signed the Declaration of Independence. At the time, George Washington was leading troops in New York, and when a copy of the declaration arrived, Washington had it read out loud to the soldiers.

had merely decided to move the battle to a different location. Their choice was New York.

Washington's forces, now expanded from the addition of militia from several other colonies, made the long march to New York, arriving in April 1776. Then they waited, trying to determine when and where the British would attack. In July, just as British warships sailed into New York's harbor, news reached Washington that the Congress meeting in Philadelphia had voted at last for independence from England. A copy of the Declaration of Independence arrived, and Washington ordered that it be read out loud to every unit in his army.

Washington's forces numbered no more than 19,000 volunteers, many of them untrained and inexperienced in the realities of battle. They were facing a British force of 32,000 highly skilled soldiers. The British attacked in August, pushing Washington's forces back from their position in Brooklyn Heights. Washington's army retreated to Manhattan, where they prepared to defend the city.

On September 15, the British invaded Manhattan. Washington heard the sound of guns being fired. When he rode toward the noise, he discovered his men running in panic. He tried his best to rally them, even threatening to kill them himself if they didn't return to their posts, but it did no good. The gunfire had been from British guns; his men had spotted the British and ran away without firing a single shot.

THE TIDE TURNS

The defeat in New York would mark the beginning of one of the darkest periods in the Revolutionary War, a time when it seemed that the rebellion against England would quickly be crushed by a superior military force. Washington's forces retreated south through New Jersey, losing men all along the way. Some were captured by the British; others were killed or wounded. Still more fell ill to smallpox or other diseases. Others chose to desert their posts or not to re-enlist when their terms of service ended.

At the end of 1776, Washington's forces—now

numbering only about 3,000—had been pushed back from New Jersey, across the Delaware River to Philadelphia. It seemed that Philadelphia—the place where independence had been declared—would soon be captured by British forces. The members of the Congress, fearing the worst, fled to Baltimore.

British General Howe, feeling confident that time was on his side, decided to pause for the winter. He set up a winter camp in New Jersey, with a Hessian outpost in Trenton. It was there that Washington struck the blow that marked a turning point in the war, launching a surprise attack as the year drew to a close. He won another victory in Princeton in January, and the British were forced back to New York.

Washington's victories were critical to the revolution. As his army marched back through New Jersey, across the land over which they had so recently retreated, they were cheered as heroes. Volunteers who had been tempted to quit the army chose to re-enlist, and new volunteers came forward. The successes encouraged France to help arm the Continental Army.

The fighting continued throughout 1777. The British were able to capture Philadelphia in September and defeat Washington's forces in decisive battles at Brandywine and Germantown, two towns in Pennsylvania, but the British decision to take Philadelphia left their forces split. American forces under General Horatio Gates attacked them at Saratoga in New York in October, ultimately defeating and capturing the 6,000-man British division.

VALLEY FORGE

Washington's forces had retired to their winter camp after a defeat at Germantown. They camped outside Philadelphia in the hills of Valley Forge, where they spent a harsh winter battling cold, sickness, and hunger. The army lacked critical supplies—many of the soldiers had no shoes for their march through the snow and no blankets to help shield them from the cold at night. Almost one out of every four men died before that winter ended.

"I am now convinced, beyond a doubt that unless some great and capital change suddenly takes place . . . this Army must inevitably be reduced to one or other of these three things. Starve, dissolve, or disperse, in order to obtain subsistence in the best manner they can. . . .

"Three or four days bad weather would prove our destruction. What then is to become of the Army this Winter? And if we are as often without Provisions now . . . what is to become of us in the Spring. . . ."

— Washington, in a letter dated December 23, 1777 from Valley Forge to the president of the Congress, begging him for the supplies his army desperately needed

Washington urged the Congress to provide the men with the supplies they desperately needed. Otherwise, he informed them, the army had only three choices: starve, dissolve, or disperse.

Help finally came— not from the Congress but from France. The French had secretly supplied the Americans with some weapons, but early in 1778, France officially announced that it would support the American struggle for independence, joining the fighting against the British.

The news helped rally Washington's troops. The

British forces left Philadelphia in June 1778, and Washington's army followed them back across New Jersey and up to New York. It was as if the clocks had turned back: Once again the British withdrew to New York, and once again Washington's troops waited outside the city.

This situation would continue for nearly three years. Small battles yielded little for either side. This stalemate was difficult for Washington. His troops again needed basic supplies and clothing. Washington pleaded with the Congress for more money, but there was none to be had. It is important to remember that the Congress represented a loose union of individual colonies. There was no nation, and so no system in place to raise national funds to support the army.

BENEDICT ARNOLD

One of the bitterest blows of the war for Washington came not from the British but from a man he considered a friend. Just after the British withdrawal from Philadelphia, Major General Benedict Arnold was selected by Washington to command the army based in that city. Arnold had fought bravely in Saratoga and had been seriously wounded there.

While in Philadelphia, Arnold met and married a young woman named Peggy Shippen. The Shippen family had chosen a neutral position in the conflict between the British and Patriots, but many in Philadelphia believed that they were secretly sympathetic to the British. Arnold's marriage to Peggy Shippen caused his loyalties to come under suspicion, and matters were made worse when it was learned that Arnold had misused public property for his own gain.

Benedict Arnold became the most famous traitor in history when he sold out West Point, which he commanded, for $20,000. One day before the British were to attack West Point, Washington learned of the plan when a message from Arnold to the British was intercepted. Arnold escaped to an English ship.

At one point, Arnold had hoped for a military promotion for his courage on the battlefield; now he was facing a court martial. By the time the decision of the court martial was made final—charging him with mishandling of public property—Arnold had begun secret talks with the British high command. The British wanted to capture West Point on the Hudson River in New York; Arnold approached George Washington and asked to be given command of that post. Washington agreed, hoping to help his friend clear his name.

Arnold, however, had become a traitor, agreeing to sell out the West Point base in exchange for $20,000.

Washington learned of Arnold's actions in September 1780, one day before the British were to have taken West Point, when a messenger carrying a note from Arnold to the British was intercepted. West Point was saved from attack, and Arnold managed to escape to the safety of a British warship.

SURRENDER AT YORKTOWN

In 1781, frustrated at their inability to win decisive victories in the northern colonies, the British turned their focus south. They attacked Georgia and South Carolina and then invaded Virginia.

British forces soon occupied the port village of Yorktown, a short distance from Williamsburg, Virginia's capital city. Then Washington received the news he had been hoping for: French ships were sailing toward the colonies to help the American cause. Washington ordered his forces of 7,000 men to march from New York to Virginia.

In late September of 1781, the American and French forces surrounded the British at Yorktown. The British forces, commanded by Lord Charles Cornwallis, were soon crushed. On the morning of October 17, Washington was writing at his desk when a messenger arrived from Cornwallis, carrying a note proposing to discuss the terms of surrender.

Although the Continental Army was posted throughout the colonies for two more years, the surrender at Yorktown effectively marked the end of the Revolutionary War.

Lord Cornwallis, the British commander, surrendered at Yorktown in late September of 1781, after the British forces were surrounded and badly defeated. The surrender was the true end of the war, although Continental forces remained posted throughout the colonies for two more years.

CRIES FOR REBELLION

As peace negotiations dragged on, many of Washington's soldiers grew angry. The war had ended, but they were still forced to remain in military camps until diplomats in Paris decided to make the end official. The threat of mutiny began to spread as soldiers issued demands for back pay and the pensions they had been promised. Many of Washington's own officers led the mutiny.

His officers' involvement worried Washington. He had not fought the war only to install a military dictatorship in its place. One of the officers had even suggested to Washington that he should become king of the new country, an offer that Washington angrily refused.

The rebellion grew stronger, and some officers began to discuss the possibility of marching to Philadelphia and demanding action from Congress. Washington learned of the plot and called for a meeting of all officers. There, Washington spoke about the "unmilitary" nature of the protest, and urged them to have faith in Congress. To show that they still had Congress' support, Washington produced a letter from a member of Virginia's delegation.

Washington began to read from the letter but then paused. Reaching into his pocket, he pulled out his reading glasses. "Gentlemen, you must pardon me," he said, looking up. "I have grown gray in your service and now find myself growing blind."

The officers were moved. With a simple gesture, Washington had once more led his men—by his dedication and by his own sacrifice. The rebellion ended. A few days later, word arrived that an agreement had been reached in Paris.

On December 23, 1783, Washington appeared before the Congress in Philadelphia to officially resign his commission. Then he left for home. He had promised his wife that he would spend Christmas with her at Mount Vernon, and as the sun was setting on Christmas Eve, Washington rode up to the outskirts of his plantation.

It had been 10 years since the Boston Tea Party had launched the colonists' struggle for independence, but now General Washington could relax. He was retiring, satisfied that the new nation was strong. His public life was over, and Washington was happy to be home at last.

THE NEW GOVERNMENT

UPON HIS RETURN home, Washington's priority was Mount Vernon. He had been away from his farm for eight years. Before leaving, he had given detailed instructions for renovations that were to be done to his home, but he discovered that much work remained.

Washington focused on his home and on his farm, encouraging his workers to experiment with different soil types and different styles of agriculture. Washington was one of the first farmers in his part of Virginia to test out a new mechanical seed spreader, one copied from a design he had found in an agricultural publication.

Washington presided over the Constitutional Convention, which met in Philadelphia from May to September of 1787. The convention was intended to revise the Articles of Confederation, but another Virginia delegate, James Madison, had a different plan that developed into the Constitution.

In May of 1787, a convention was scheduled to meet in Philadelphia, where delegates would discuss how the various states could come together to form some system of federal government. Washington was elected to serve as one of the delegates from Virginia. He refused the nomination.

Washington strongly believed in the value of a strong national government. His experience during the war had taught him that the separate colonies had certain common needs and shared values, all of which would benefit from a stronger national government.

Still, Washington was reluctant to return to a public role. He enjoyed his life at Mount Vernon. He was 55 years old and suffering from rheumatism. Like many people in those days, he has lost most of his teeth, which made him self-conscious about public speaking.

Many of the leading men in Virginia came to visit Washington, insisting that his presence would be vital to the convention. After months of discussions, he finally was persuaded to accept.

THE CONSTITUTIONAL CONVENTION

The convention that began that hot summer of 1787 in Philadelphia had a critical role: to help ensure that the union of states, which had survived a war, could continue to survive and thrive after that war. A total of 55 delegates, representing every state but Rhode Island, gathered in the very same building—the Pennsylvania State House—where George Washington had been named the commander of the Continental Army. Now, 12 years later, Washington was given another appointment: He was elected the president of the convention.

In addition to Washington, the Virginia delegation contained another important figure: 36-year-old James Madison. Madison had helped the Virginia delegation draft a dramatic proposal for the future of the union that was presented to the convention on May 29, 1787. Known as the "Virginia Plan," the proposal contained the framework for a new system of government quite different from the competitive collection of states that had arisen after British rule ended.

The new government would be a national system with a strong central government of officials elected by the people. It would contain three branches: executive, legislative, and judicial.

This was a radical proposal. The convention had gathered to revise the Articles of Confederation, agreed to in 1777 and ratified in 1781, which had previously governed dealings between the states (the colonies had also become known as "states" with the passage of the Articles of Confederation). Now the group from Virginia, with Washington's support, was proposing to toss aside what had been set up since the war and create a brand-new system of government, unlike any other that existed at that time. Rather than quickly shouting down the proposal, the delegates voted to support it.

Disagreements arose among the delegates about exactly how representatives should be elected and how the different states would be represented in this new form of government. Delegates from smaller, less populous states felt that each state should receive the same number of votes, whereas those from larger states felt that representation should be proportional (based on population). This obstacle was resolved by creating two legislative branches: a Senate, in which each state would have the same number of representatives, and a House of Representatives, in which the number of representatives from each state would be determined by population.

A second debate was sparked by discussions over the executive branch. Given their recent experience as subjects of a monarchy, it is not surprising that many of the delegates were not in favor of giving too much power to any one person. There were many proposals: an executive branch containing three individuals; a president who was appointed by the legislative branch or the judicial branch; a president who could be recalled; a president who could be impeached by the individual states; a president who was responsible only for domestic affairs and not foreign policy; a president who was not commander in chief of the military; and a president who could only serve one term.

George Washington brought an end to these proposals, not by his words (as president of the convention, he did not speak during the debates) but instead by

The Constitution was signed by 39 delegates of the Constitutional Convention on September 17, 1787. One of the country's first acts was to create the electoral college, which then elected George Washington as president in a process that was clearly outlined in the Constitution.

his presence. Pierce Butler, one of the delegates from South Carolina, noted, "Members cast their eyes toward General Washington as President, and shaped their ideas of the power to be given to a President, by their opinions of his virtue." In the end, the delegates voted for a strong and independent executive branch, creating the role with George Washington very much in mind.

On September 17, 1787, a constitution based on the principles discussed at the convention was signed by 39 delegates. The document began with the stirring words "We the people of the United States," but the people were hardly united in the early days of the nation's history. In fact, one of the few points upon which most citizens agreed was their choice for their first president: George Washington.

THE PRESIDENT OF THE UNITED STATES

The system for choosing a president had been outlined carefully in the Constitution. An electoral college would be created, containing electors chosen by each of the states. Each elector would have two votes—and each of his votes must go to a different candidate. Perhaps even more astonishing to modern readers, the candidate receiving the most votes would become president and the candidate in second place would become vice president.

The members of the electoral college were chosen in January 1789. In those days, there were no political campaigns or political parties to nominate candidates. To no one's surprise, Washington was the unanimous choice of the electoral college—every elector cast one of his votes for George Washington. John Adams was elected vice president.

On April 14, 1789, Washington was officially informed of his election, and two days later he left Mount Vernon for the capital—at that time located in New York City. His journey north was marked by celebrations all along the route. Bells rang and cannons boomed in every city through which he passed. When he reached New York, a crowd of 30,000 people welcomed him. Washington crossed the Hudson River into Manhattan on a specially built barge, with decorated boats trailing behind him. When he reached Manhattan, Washington walked past adoring citizens who threw flowers at his feet.

> "The event which I have long dreaded, I am at last constrained to believe, is now likely to happen. For that I have during many months, been oppressed with an apprehension it might be deemed unavoidably expedient for me to go again into public life, is known to all, who know me. But from the moment, when the necessity had become more apparent, and as it were inevitable, I anticipated, in a heart filled with distress, the ten thousand embarrassments, perplexities and troubles to which I must again be exposed in the evening of a life, already nearly consumed in public cares."
>
> — Washington, in a letter written from Mount Vernon on March 21, 1789, expressing his reluctance to leave home to become president as he awaits the official notification of his election by the electoral college

The celebrating continued for several days. The inauguration was delayed until April 30, in part to accommodate all of the festivities and in part because an important question remained to be settled: Exactly what would the nation call its new leader? Among the proposals was "His Highness the President of

PRESIDENT WASHINGTON'S LEGACY

Shaping the Presidency

When the executive branch of the United States government was first created by the Constitutional Convention in 1789, many of its functions were designed with George Washington in mind. It was commonly assumed that he would be the first leader of this new executive branch, and so certain responsibilities—for example, that the president would also serve as commander in chief of the armed forces—were included in the executive branch's powers.

Because George Washington was the first president, many of his actions became the practice of succeeding presidents. Washington created the very first president's cabinet; it contained four men. He set the precedent of presidents traveling around the country and appointed the first 10 justices of the Supreme Court.

Washington assumed that the president would shape both domestic and foreign policy. His active involvement in these two areas helped create the assertive role future presidents would take in foreign policy and contributed to the establishment of a strong and independent executive branch.

Finally, Washington established the precedent of a president serving no more than two terms—a precedent broken only by Franklin Roosevelt, who served three. In fact, Washington had wanted to serve only one term but reluctantly agreed to serve a second. Given Washington's immense popularity, it seems certain that he could have been elected president for life. The United States might have developed quite differently if each of its presidents viewed his election as a lifetime appointment.

the United States of America and Protector of Their Liberties." Finally, the matter was settled: He would be called simply "The President of the United States."

6

THE FIRST PRESIDENT

ON APRIL 30, 1789, the first president of the United States was inaugurated. It was a day of tremendous celebration in New York City. At dawn, artillery blasted out from the battery. At 9:00 A.M., the sound of church bells rang through the city, announcing the start of prayer services. At noon, the members of Congress gathered and then sent official representatives to the place where Washington was staying to escort him to the ceremony. The parade then marched back to Federal Hall: five military divisions first, then the mayor and sheriff of New York on horseback, and then the representatives from the Senate all squeezed into a single horse-drawn carriage. Next came Washington, riding alone in a large carriage drawn by four

George Washington was inaugurated on April 30, 1789, in New York City, then the capital of the United States. Washington took his oath at Federal Hall, on the corner of Broad and Wall Streets, then stepped inside to make a formal address to officials.

horses. Then came the delegation from the House of Representatives, again all squeezed into a single carriage, followed by various other local officials.

The ceremony began at about 1:00 P.M. Washington greeted John Adams, his vice president, and Adams then made a brief speech to the assembled officials. Then

Washington stepped out onto a balcony above Broad and Wall Streets. There he took his oath of office as the crowds below cheered.

Washington stepped back inside and, standing before the gathered officials, he gave his inaugural address. A friend had prepared a 73-page speech, but fortunately for those in attendance, Washington had instead decided to give a much briefer speech, only seven paragraphs long. About 20 minutes after it had begun, the inauguration was over. The United States had its first president.

A REVOLUTIONARY TIME

George Washington's new task was to lead a nation that had undergone dramatic changes. It had been transformed from a collection of British colonies into a series of loosely connected states and then again to a unified single nation. The nation had a written constitution and a new system of government.

Many of the details of

"Among the vicissitudes incident to life, no event could have filled me with greater anxieties than that of which the notification was transmitted by your order [informing him that he had been elected president] . . . . On the one hand, I was summoned by my Country, whose voice I can never hear but with veneration and love . . . . On the other hand, the magnitude and difficulty of the trust to which the voice of my Country called me, being sufficient to awaken in the wisest and most experienced of her citizens, a distrustful scrutiny into his qualifications, could not but overwhelm with dispondence, one, who inheriting inferior endowments from nature and unpracticed in the duties of civil administration, ought to be peculiarly conscious of his own deficiencies."

— Washington, from his inaugural address on April 30, 1789, in New York City. The tone is quite different from the inaugural addresses given by modern presidents that new system of government remained to be spelled out in greater detail. Washington's role as the first president helped influence decisions that gave additional strength to the executive branch. In one example, Congress voted that three important departments of the government—the departments of treasury, state, and war—would come under the control of the president. He would have the power to nominate the heads (or "secretaries") of each of those departments who would then be confirmed by the Senate, and he would retain the power to remove those secretaries without consulting the Senate.

For these first important positions, Washington chose men whom he knew well. Thomas Jefferson was named secretary of state. Henry Knox was chosen as secretary of war. Alexander Hamilton was named secretary of the treasury—the position that George Washington felt was the most important within his cabinet. These three influential and intelligent men seemed wise choices, but they had very different views of what shape the new nation should take. Their disagreements would create trouble for Washington and later for the nation itself.

Washington began the tradition of presidents shaping foreign policy. The Constitution had not been clear on this point, stating only that treaties with other nations would be made "by and with the Advice and Consent of the Senate." How this was to happen was never spelled out. On August 22, 1789, Washington visited the Senate chamber to discuss a pending treaty with a tribe of Creek Indians. After a lengthy reading of the proposed treaty, the Senate asked to postpone their decision until they could study the documents. Washington was not pleased. Two days later, he returned to the Senate for additional debate. He left vowing never to return—and he kept his promise. Neither Washington nor any of the presidents who followed him would go to the Senate to negotiate another treaty. In future, presidents would draft the treaties and the Senate would be responsible only for deciding whether or not to ratify them.

POLITICAL PARTIES FORM

During Washington's term, two different groups began to form among political thinkers and activists. At the head of each group were members of Washington's own cabinet: Alexander Hamilton and Thomas Jefferson. To Washington's horror, these groups soon formed distinct political parties.

Thomas Jefferson's followers defined themselves as Democratic-Republicans but were often simply called "Republicans." They viewed America principally as a nation of farmers and saw their new nation as an agricultural society. They supported a limited role for the national government and felt that the individual states should retain strong powers to keep government small and local.

Alexander Hamilton and his supporters viewed America in quite a different way. They felt that America needed a strong central government with a federal government more powerful than the individual states. They called themselves Federalists. In their view, America would become a nation of big cities and big business, equal in power to the nations of Europe.

These two groups' political views led them to support quite different approaches to foreign policy. Jefferson and the Republicans applauded revolutionaries' overthrow of the French aristocracy and argued for forming stronger ties with the government that took the place of the French monarchy. Hamilton and the Federalists viewed with horror the bloody violence that had brought about the French Revolution and thought that America should retain strong ties with Britain.

The conflict erupted when Hamilton, as secretary of the treasury, announced his plan to resolve the outstanding debts many of the states (mostly northern states) still owed from the Revolutionary War. Hamilton's plan involved the federal government assuming responsibility for the states' war debts and it spoke of a new bank of the United States, which would issue paper money; Hamilton's plan also talked of investments and taxation.

Jefferson and the Republicans were furious at these plans. Representatives from the powerful state of Virginia were particularly angry. Virginia had paid off its war debt. Why should it be penalized and forced to help pay off the debts of the northern states?

Finally, a compromise was reached. Southerners agreed to support the new financial plan in exchange for an important concession. The new national capital would not be located in New York or Philadelphia. It would be based in the South, at a point along the Potomac River, where a new city would be built to serve as a fitting site for government. In the meantime, the capital would be relocated from New York to Philadelphia until the city could be constructed.

George Washington quickly became a supporter of the decision to relocate the government near Virginia. He himself picked the site, a location only a short distance from Mount Vernon.

PRESIDENT WASHINGTON'S LEGACY

Washington, D.C.

The city of Washington, D.C., is an important part of George Washington's legacy. His influence extends beyond its name. When it was decided that the new capital city would be located along the Potomac River, Washington helped ensure that the capital would be located within a short distance of his home in northern Virginia.

Washington also selected the engineer who would give the city its distinctive design. Pierre Charles L'Enfant was a French architect and engineer who had joined Washington's army during the Revolutionary War and rose to the rank of major. Washington admired L'Enfant's design of the city hall in New York and agreed to allow him to prepare a design for the new capital. At the time, the 10-mile area that had been designated for the capital was largely undeveloped, giving designers an opportunity to create a city almost from scratch. L'Enfant's design featured ceremonial open spaces and grand, diagonal avenues that radiated out from the two most important building sites—the places where the President's House and the Congress would be located. The design symbolically showed power flowing out from these two points. L'Enfant had specified wide avenues, lined with trees, that would connect certain sites throughout the city— points at which important monuments or structures were to be built. Washington liked L'Enfant's plan and lobbied hard for it to be chosen. The city of Washington, D.C., stands today much as L'Enfant and Washington first pictured it more than 200 years ago.

He also helped to select the man who would design the new city. Thomas Jefferson had become involved in the project, drafting his own plans for the designs of federal buildings. Washington, however, liked the Federal Hall building in New York, and its architect, a 37-year-old former officer in the Continental Army named Pierre Charles L'Enfant, was ultimately selected to serve as the project engineer. L'Enfant's design was approved, and construction of the new capital began.

A RELUCTANT EXECUTIVE

By May 1792, Washington had decided not to serve a second term as president. He had suffered through two serious illnesses and was entering his 60s. Washington felt that he did not have many years left, and he wanted to spend them at Mount Vernon.

In addition, Washington had been troubled by the growing split between Jefferson and Hamilton. Spurred on by the growing competition between the two political viewpoints, newspapers had become increasingly critical of Washington's administration. Washington told James Madison that he wanted to retire and asked him for his help in preparing a farewell address.

Madison agreed to help, but as they worked together, he argued with Washington about the need for him to remain in office. The divisions between Hamilton and Jefferson were reflecting a wide split in political opinion in the country as a whole. If George Washington were to step down, the resulting presidential election would emphasize

Washington chose men that he knew well as his cabinet members. He considered the secretary of the treasury to be the most important position and chose Alexander Hamilton (middle) for it. Thomas Jefferson (second from right) was the secretary of state, meaning that he dealt in foreign affairs. The other men in the picture are, from left, Washington, Secretary of War Henry Knox, and Attorney General Edmund Randolph.

this split and result in a bitter election process. For the good of the country, Madison urged, Washington must stay on as president.

As he continued to insist that he would serve only one term, Washington spent part of the summer of 1792 considering proposed designs for what would become the "President's House" in the new capital. Both L'Enfant and Jefferson had submitted their own designs, but Washington's choice was a design by James Hoban, an Irish emigrant who had patterned his design after a classical English architectural scheme. Washington's recommendation was approved, and work on the structure that would become the White House began.

Washington ultimately agreed to serve another term as president, writing to both Jefferson and Hamilton to urge them to stop their quarrel or the country would be torn apart. In 1793, the electoral college once again unanimously elected George Washington. John Adams was also re-elected vice president.

SECOND TERM DIFFICULTIES

Although splits within the country worried Washington as he reluctantly began his second term, his attention soon turned to divisions sparked by foreign events. In 1793, war broke out between England and the revolutionary government in France. The war served to once more emphasize the divisions within America. Washington issued an official Proclamation of Neutrality, but Jefferson and the Republicans made their support for France clear, whereas Hamilton and the Federalists sided with England.

Critical newspapers had accused Washington of wanting to become "king of America" and of taking advantage of the perks of office to live lavishly. The charge was untrue, but the fact that Washington did not speak strongly in support of France in the conflict added to the rumors. Washington was charged with siding with England because he felt he had more in common with a king than with revolutionaries.

Washington's choice—to remain neutral in the conflict

between England and France—was not a scheme to secretly support one side or the other. He believed that America needed time to become a strong, unified country and that involvement in the war could spark a civil war as well.

The Proclamation of Neutrality did not protect American ships, which were attacked by both England and France. Pro-French groups formed and began speaking out to encourage American support of the French cause. Washington spoke out strongly against the groups, causing Thomas Jefferson to resign from his cabinet.

Washington finally negotiated a treaty with England to avoid war and ensure the safety of American ships. The treaty caused intense debate within the Senate and House, where Washington was accused of giving in to the British. The treaty was ultimately ratified, but its passage cost Washington.

Newspapers that had supported the pro-French Republican cause attacked Washington. He was called a tyrant and described as old and senile, and even his former supporter, Thomas Paine, turned on him. "You commenced your Presidential career by encouraging, and swallowing the grossest adulation," Paine wrote in a pamphlet entitled *Letter to George Washington.* ". . . As to you, sir, treacherous in private friendship . . . and a hypocrite in public life, the world will be puzzled to decide, whether you have abandoned good principles, or whether you ever had any."

It was a terrible blow to Washington to have remained in office only at the urging of others and then to find his decisions sharply criticized. In the spring of 1796, he firmly decided that his second term would be his last. He took the farewell address that James Madison had helped him create a few years earlier and this time sent it on to Alexander Hamilton, who had left the cabinet in 1795. Hamilton added his comments and, in September 1796, Washington's farewell address was published.

With the address, Washington made his farewell official, but six months of his second term still remained. He spent one of those months at Mount Vernon and the remainder in the temporary capital of Philadelphia. He was a witness to the first fiercely fought presidential election. The Republicans had chosen Thomas Jefferson to represent their cause; the Federalists' choice was Vice President John Adams. Washington chose to stay out of the election, refusing to support one or the other candidate. It was a close election; John Adams won with a tiny majority of three electoral votes.

"The Unity of Government which constitutes you one people is also now dear to you. It is justly so; for it is a main Pillar in the Edifice of your real independence, the support of your tranquility at home; your peace abroad; of your safety; of your prosperity; of that very Liberty which you so highly prize. . . .

The name of AMERICAN, which belongs to you, in your national capacity, must always exalt the just pride of Patriotism . . . . With slight shades of difference, you have the same Religion, Manners, Habits and political Principles. You have in a common cause fought and triumphed together. The independence and liberty you possess are the work of joint councils, and joint efforts; of common dangers, sufferings and successes. . . ."

— Washington, in his farewell address published on September 17, 1796. In it, he outlined his hopes for the nation and his hopes that the office he was leaving had helped to produce a strong, unified country

FINAL RECOMMENDATIONS

During his final days in office, Washington made several recommendations, actions that he hoped would be taken as a kind of legacy. He urged the creation of a military academy where the nation's officers could be trained. He urged that the militia system be reformed to create a national militia rather than the system of individual militias for each state that existed. He pleaded for a pay raise for army officers and suggested the creation of a United States navy and a national university.

On March 4, 1797, John Adams was inaugurated as the second president of the United States. The new president wrote to his wife that Washington himself was the only one who seemed happy at the change in leadership: "Methought I heard him say, 'Ay! I am fairly out and you fairly in! See which of us will be happiest!'" A few days later, their belongings packed, George and Martha Washington left for home.

MOUNT VERNON AT LAST

When Washington returned to Mount Vernon, he immediately set to work overseeing necessary repairs and upgrades to the various buildings on his plantation. Washington had brought with him the art he had collected as president, as well as several volumes of writings that made up his presidential papers. He began to consider the possibility of creating a kind of presidential library, where his writings could be displayed, on the grounds of Mount Vernon.

Washington also focused again on the issue of slavery,

Washington retired to Mount Vernon after his presidency. A slave-owner for most of his life, the issue began to trouble Washington more and more after he left the presidency. Many of the slaves at Mount Vernon were set free upon his death, and the rest were freed when Martha died. The younger ones were taught a trade and to read and write. The older ones, unable to care for themselves, were to be supported by Washington's heirs.

a concern that had troubled him for some time. Although he had suggested many years earlier that the practice of slavery might be abolished, he had taken no decisive steps to do so himself and had continued to buy and sell slaves.

At the end of his presidency, Washington left several slaves behind in Philadelphia, giving them their freedom. During his remaining days in Mount Vernon, Washington took more decisive steps to free all of his slaves. In his will, he stated that some of his slaves would be set free upon his death, and the remainder would be set free either upon his or Martha's death, depending on who outlived the other. Infants and young children were to be taught a craft and to read and write, so that in freedom they could support themselves. Those slaves too old or sick to care for themselves were to be fed, clothed, and sheltered by Washington's heirs.

Even in retirement, Washington continued to face pressure to return to public service. In 1789, when war with France threatened, President Adams appointed George Washington as commander of the new army of the United States. This brief service led again to suggestions that he should seek a third presidential term. Washington refused.

On December 12, 1799, Washington was keeping to his habit of riding around the grounds of Mount Vernon to inspect his farm. The grounds were covered with snow, and it continued to snow as he rode around the estate for several hours. When he returned, he complained of a sore throat, and it continued to bother him the next day. In the middle of the night on December 13, Washington woke again, feeling very ill. He could barely speak and was having trouble breathing.

Several doctors were quickly called to Mount Vernon, but there was little that could be done. Washington knew that he was dying. Despite his pain, he continued to give orders to his doctors and aides up until his last moment. At about 10:30 P.M. on December 14, 1799, 67-year-old George Washington took his own pulse. He then relaxed and died.

A NATION MOURNS

When George Washington died, the national government that he had helped to shape was only 10 years old. The Constitution was only 12 years old. George Washington had been, in many ways, the symbol that held 13 separate colonies together and enabled them to form a single unified country.

In his death, the nation was once again unified, this time in grief. Those who had criticized Washington the president now were silenced at the outpouring of sadness at the loss of Washington the hero.

Washington had understood his legacy well. He knew that as the nation's first president, he would be studied and imitated by those who followed. He knew that each step he took would become a precedent and that his actions and words would inevitably shape the office of president of the United States.

This is where his leadership can be most clearly seen and why we remember him today as one of our greatest presidents. He did not choose to set himself up as king, although many urged him to do so. He chose to put America's interests first—often above his own. He took steps to create a strong nation, understanding that the nation must be strong enough to survive without him. When the time came, Washington chose to step down and allow others to lead the nation, leaving behind him a legacy that has guided every president, and the entire nation, for over 200 years.

THE PRESIDENTS
OF THE
UNITED STATES

George Washington
1789–1797

John Adams
1797–1801

Thomas Jefferson
1801–1809

James Madison
1809–1817

James Monroe
1817–1825

John Quincy Adams
1825–1829

Andrew Jackson
1829–1837

Martin Van Buren
1837–1841

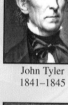

William Henry
Harrison
1841

John Tyler
1841–1845

James Polk
1845–1849

Zachary Taylor
1849–1850

Millard Filmore
1850–1853

Franklin Pierce
1853–1857

James Buchanan
1857–1861

Abraham Lincoln
1861–1865

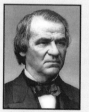

Andrew Johnson
1865–1869

Ulysses S. Grant
1869–1877

Rutherford B. Hayes
1877–1881

James Garfield
1881

Chester Arthur
1881–1885

Grover Cleveland
1885–1889

Benjamin Harrison
1889–1893

Grover Cleveland
1893-1897

William McKinley
1897–1901

Theodore Roosevelt
1901–1909

William H. Taft
1909–1913

Woodrow Wilson
1913–1921

Warren Harding
1921–1923

Calvin Coolidge
1923–1929

Herbert Hoover
1929–1933

Franklin D. Roosevelt 1933–1945

Harry S. Truman
1945–1953

Dwight Eisenhower
1953–1961

John F. Kennedy
1961–1963

Lyndon Johnson
1963–1969

Richard Nixon
1969–1974

Gerald Ford
1974–1977

Jimmy Carter
1977–1981

Ronald Reagan
1981–1989

George H.W. Bush
1989–1993

William J. Clinton
1993–2001

George W. Bush
2001–

Note: Dates indicate years of
presidential service.
Source: www.whitehouse.gov

Presidential Fact File

THE CONSTITUTION

Article II of the Constitution of the United States outlines several requirements for the president of the United States, including:

★ **Age:** The president must be at least 35 years old.

★ **Citizenship:** The president must be a U.S. citizen.

★ **Residency:** The president must have lived in the United States for at least 14 years.

★ **Oath of Office:** On his inauguration, the president takes this oath: "I do solemnly swear (or affirm) that I will faithfully execute the office of President of the United States, and will to the best of my ability, preserve, protect and defend the Constitution of the United States."

★ **Term:** A presidential term lasts four years.

PRESIDENTIAL POWERS

The president has many distinct powers as outlined in and interpreted from the Constitution. The president:

★ Submits many proposals to Congress for regulatory, social, and economic reforms.

★ Appoints federal judges with the Senate's approval.

★ Prepares treaties with foreign nations to be approved by the Senate.

★ Can veto laws passed by Congress.

★ Acts as commander in chief of the military to oversee military strategy and actions.

★ Appoints members of the cabinet and many other agencies and administrations with the Senate's approval.

★ Can declare martial law (control of local governments within the country) in times of national crisis.

Presidential Fact File

TRADITION

Many parts of the presidency developed out of tradition. The traditions listed below are but a few that are associated with the U.S. presidency.

★ After taking his oath of office, George Washington added, "So help me God." Numerous presidents since Washington have also added this phrase to their oath.

★ Originally, the Constitution limited the term of the presidency to four years, but did not limit the number of terms a president could serve. Presidents, following the precedent set by George Washington, traditionally served only two terms. After Franklin Roosevelt was elected to four terms, however, Congress amended the Constitution to restrict presidents to only two.

★ James Monroe was the first president to have his inauguration outside the Capitol. From his inauguration in 1817 to Jimmy Carter's inauguration in 1977, it was held on the Capitol's east portico. Ronald Reagan broke from this tradition in 1981 when he was inaugurated on the west portico to face his home state, California. Since 1981, all presidential inaugurations have been held on the west portico of the Capitol.

★ Not all presidential traditions are serious, however. One of the more fun activities connected with the presidency began when President William Howard Taft ceremoniously threw out the first pitch of the new baseball season in 1910.  Presidents since Taft have carried on this tradition, including Woodrow Wilson, who is pictured here as he throws the first pitch of the 1916 season. In more recent years, the president has also opened the All-Star and World Series games.

PRESIDENTIAL FACT FILE

THE WHITE HOUSE

Although George Washington was involved with the planning of the White House, he never lived there. It has been, however, the official residence of every president beginning with John Adams, the second U.S. president. The building was completed approximately in 1800, although it has undergone several renovations since then. It was the first public building constructed in Washington, D.C. The White House has 132 rooms, several of which are open to the public. Private rooms include those for administration and the president's personal residence. For an online tour of the White House and other interesting facts, visit the official White House website, *http://www.whitehouse.gov*.

THE PRESIDENTIAL SEAL

A committee began planning the presidential seal in 1777. It was completed in 1782. The seal appears as an official stamp on medals, stationery, and documents, among other items. Originally, the eagle faced right toward the

arrows (a symbol of war) that it held in its talons. In 1945, President Truman had the seal altered so that the eagle's head instead faced left toward the olive branch (a symbol of peace), because he believed the president should be prepared for war but always look toward peace.

PRESIDENT WASHINGTON IN PROFILE

PERSONAL

Name: George Washington

Birth date: February 11, 1732 (after the calendar change, February 22)

Birth place: Westmoreland County, Virginia

Father: Augustine Washington

Mother: Mary Ball

Wife: Martha Dandridge Custis

Children: John Parke Custis (adopted) and Martha Custis (adopted)

Death date: December 14, 1799

Death place: Mount Vernon, Virginia

POLITICAL

Years in office: 1789–1797

Vice president: John Adams

Occupations before presidency: Planter, surveyor, mason, and soldier

Political party: Federalist

Major achievements of presidency: Developed the office of the presidency

Nickname: The Father of Our Country

Presidential library:
The George Washington Papers at the Library of Congress
Manuscript Division
Library of Congress
101 Independence Avenue, SE
Washington, D.C. 20540-4680
Interoffice Mail: LS/PSCD/MSS (4680)
(202) 707-5383

Tributes:

George Washington Memorial Parkway
(McLean, Va.; *http://www.nps.gov/gwmp*)

Moland House Park
(Warwick, Pa.; *http://moland.org*)

Mount Rushmore National Memorial
(Keystone, S.D.; *http://www.nps.gov/moru/*)

Mount Vernon
(Mount Vernon, Va.; *http://www.mountvernon.org*)

Historic Valley Forge
(Valley Forge, Pa.; *http://www.ushistory.org/valleyforge/*)

Washington Monument
(Washington, D.C.; *http://www.nps.gov/wamo/*)

George Washington Birthplace
(Westmoreland County, Va.; *http://www.nps.gov/gewa/*)

George Washington National Masonic Memorial
(Alexandria, Va.; *http://www.gwmemorial.org/*)

1732 George Washington is born on February 11 (a change in calendar later moves date ahead to February 22).

1748 George Washington makes his first surveying trip.

1753 Washington travels to the Ohio Valley with a message demanding the withdrawal of French troops.

1754 A small skirmish leads to French and Indian War. Washington's troops are defeated at the Forks of the Ohio.

1759 Washington marries Martha Custis.

1774 Washington represents Virginia at the First Continental Congress.

1775 Washington is named commander of the Continental Army. The Revolutionary War begins.

1776 Washington wins a victory at Trenton.

1777 The Continental Army suffers through winter at Valley Forge.

1781 The British surrender at Yorktown.

1787 Washington is named president of the Constitutional Convention.

1789 Washington is the unanimous choice of the electoral college and is elected president of the United States.

1792 Washington is re-elected president.

1797 John Adams is elected president. Washington returns to Mount Vernon.

1799 Washington dies on December 14.

BIBLIOGRAPHY

Abbot, W. W., ed. *The Papers of George Washington: Colonial Series, Vol. 1, 1748–August 1755*. Charlottesville, Va.: University Press of Virginia, 1983.

Commins, Saxe, ed. *Basic Writings of George Washington*. New York: Random House, 1948.

Ferling, John E. *The First of Men: A Life of George Washington*. Knoxville, Tenn.: The University of Tennessee Press, 1988.

Flexner, James Thomas. *George Washington: The Forge of Experience (1732–1775)*. Boston: Little, Brown & Co., 1965.

———. *Washington: The Indispensable Man*. Boston: Little, Brown & Co., 1974.

Ford, Worthington Chauncey. *George Washington*. New York: Charles Scribner's Sons, 1900.

Freeman, Douglas Southall. *George Washington: A Biography. Vol. 4: Leader of the Revolution*. New York: Charles Scribner's Sons, 1951.

———. *Washington*. New York: Macmillan Publishing Company, 1992.

Headley, J.T. *The Life of George Washington*. New York: Charles Scribner, 1856.

Jackson, Donald, ed. *The Diaries of George Washington: Volume 1, 1748–65*. Charlottesville, Va.: University Press of Virginia, 1976.

Lewis, Thomas A. *For King and Country: The Maturing of George Washington*. New York: HarperCollins Publishers, 1993.

Marshall, John. *Life of Washington. Vol. 2*. New York: Wm. H. Wise & Co., 1925.

Rhodehamel, John. *The Great Experiment: George Washington and the American Republic*. New Haven, Conn.: Yale University Press, 1998.

Smith, Richard Norton. *Patriarch: George Washington and the New American Nation*. Boston: Houghton Mifflin Co., 1993.

Twohig, Dorothy, ed. *The Papers of George Washington. Vol 7: Revolutionary War Series, October 1776–January 1777*. Charlottesville, Va.: University Press of Virginia, 1997.

BIBLIOGRAPHY

WEBSITES

American Presidents: Life Portraits
http://americanpresidents.org

The American Presidency
http://gi.grolier.com/presidents

The Papers of George Washington
http://gwpapers.virginia.edu

George Washington Papers at the Library of Congress
http://lcweb2.loc.gov/ammem/gwhtml/

George Washington's Mount Vernon: Estate & Gardens
http://mountvernon.org

The White House: The Presidents of the United States
http://whitehouse.gov/history/presidents/

Ferrie, Richard. *The World Turned Upside Down: George Washington and the Battle of Yorktown.* New York: Holiday House, 1999.

Foster, Genevieve. *George Washington's World.* New York: Charles Scribner's Sons, 1941.

Harness, Cheryl. *George Washington.* Washington, D.C.: National Geographic, 2000.

Heilbroner, Joan. *Meet George Washington.* New York: Random House, 2001.

Rhodehamel, John. *The Great Experiment: George Washington and the American Republic.* New Haven, Conn.: Yale University Press, 1998.

WEBSITES

George Washington: A National Treasure
http://www.georgewashington.si.edu/

Rediscovering George Washington
http://www.pbs.org/georgewashington/

Historic Valley Forge: George Washington
http://www.ushistory.org/valleyforge/washington/

Meet Amazing Americans: George Washington
http://www.americaslibrary.gov/cgi-bin/page.cgi/aa/wash

CIA History: George Washington
http://www.cia.gov/cia/ciakids/history/george.html

From Revolution to Reconstruction: George Washington
http://odur.let.rug.nl/~usa/P/gw1/gw1.htm

INDEX

PICTURE CREDITS

page:

11: © Bettmann/CORBIS
15: Courtesy of the Library of Congress, Geography and Map Division
19: © Associated Press, AP
23: © Bettmann/CORBIS
29: © Bettmann/CORBIS
35: Courtesy of the Library of Congress, LC-USZCN4-184
39: © Bettmann/CORBIS
44: © Hulton|Archive, by Getty Images
47: Courtesy of the Library of Congress
51: Courtesy of the Library of Congress, LC-USZC2-2711

56: © Associated Press, Library of Congress
58: Courtesy of the Library of Congress, LC-USZC2-3052
61: © Hulton|Archive, by Getty Images
65: Courtesy of the National Archives
71: © Associated Press, AP
78: Courtesy of the Library of Congress, LC-USZ62-1306
83: © CORBIS
86-87: Courtesy Library of Congress, "Portraits of the Presidents and First Ladies" American Memory Collection

Cover: © Museum of the City of New York/CORBIS

ACKNOWLEDGMENTS

Thank you to Celebrity Speakers Intl. for coordinating Mr. Cronkite's contribution to this book.

ABOUT THE CONTRIBUTORS

Heather Lehr Wagner is a writer and editor. She earned an M.A. in government from the College of William and Mary and a B.A. in political science from Duke University. She has written several books for teens on social and political issues and is the author of *John Adams, Thomas Jefferson,* and *Ronald Reagan* in the GREAT AMERICAN PRESIDENTS series.

Walter Cronkite has covered virtually every major news event during his more than 60 years in journalism, during which he earned a reputation for being "the most trusted man in America." He began his career as a reporter for the United Press during World War II, taking part in the beachhead assaults of Normandy and covering the Nuremberg trials. He then joined *CBS News* in Washington, D.C., where he was the news anchor for political convention and election coverage from 1952 to 1980. CBS debuted its first half-hour weeknight news program with Mr. Cronkite's interview of President John F. Kennedy in 1963. Mr. Cronkite was inducted into the Academy of Television Arts and Sciences in 1985 and has written several books. He lives in New York City with his wife of 63 years.